INSIDE THE COUNTRY MUSIC HALL OF FAME® AND MUSEUM

A VISITOR'S COMPANION

Country Music Foundation® Press

HONOR THY MUSIC®

www.countrymusichalloffame.com

Country Music Foundation® Press

Nashville, Tennessee 37203

Designer: LY designs/Lynette Sesler

Cover Photo: Tim Hursley

TABLE OF CONTENTS

As an active exhibition and research center, the Country Music Hall of Fame® and Museum
stages new museum displays to highlight the diverse and continually evolving history of country music.
This visitor's companion is revised frequently to reflect the Museum's dynamic exhibition schedule.
Some artifacts pictured may no longer be on display in the Museum,
and not all artifacts on display are included in this book.

HISTORY AND MISSION

Located in Nashville, Tennessee, the Country Music Hall of Fame® and Museum is a non-profit educational organization, chartered by the state of Tennessee in 1964 with a mandate to collect, preserve, and make available to the public artifacts and information relating to the history of country music.

The original museum.

The first Country Music Hall of Fame® election took place in 1961, and the plaques were temporarily displayed in Nashville's Tennessee State Museum. Country music's highest honor gained a home of its own when the Country Music Hall of Fame® and Museum became a reality. The original Museum building, located on Sixteenth Avenue on Nashville's Music Row, opened to

The Everly Brothers at RCA's Studio B.

the public on April 1, 1967. The Museum expanded operations steadily as attendance increased. A research library was opened in 1968, and building expansions took place in 1974, 1977, and 1984, which more than doubled the size of the Museum. Staff grew accordingly as the Museum developed programs in education, publications, oral history, the reissuing of historic recordings, and other areas related to museum work.

In its thirty-three enormously successful years on Music Row, the Country Music Hall of Fame® and Museum hosted more than ten million museum visitors, in addition to many more guests at after-hours functions. In 2001, to accommodate expanding collections and programs, the Country Music Hall of Fame® and Museum moved to a new location and a new building—more than four times the size of the old building—in downtown Nashville.

Located in the heart of Nashville's arts and entertainment district, the new 130,000-square-foot Country Music Hall of Fame® and Museum houses a collection encompassing close to 750,000 historical artifacts, photographs, recordings, and films. Accredited by the American Association of Museums, the Country Music Hall of Fame® and Museum is the world's largest center for country music research and collections. The Museum also operates two historic sites: RCA's Studio B, a recording studio that helped give birth to the Nashville Sound, and Hatch Show Print, a historic poster print shop with longtime ties to country music.

Throughout all its growth and changes, the essential mission of the Country Music Hall of Fame® and Museum has remained constant: *to identify and preserve the evolving history and traditions of country music and to educate its audiences. Functioning as a local history museum and as an international arts organization, the Country Music Hall of Fame® and Museum serves visiting and non-visiting audiences including fans, students, professional scholars, members of the music industry, the media, and the general public—in the Nashville area, the nation, and the world.*

Hatch Show Print, a Hall of Fame historic site.

THE MUSEUM'S ARCHITECTURAL SYMBOLISM

Your journey through the history of country music, as presented by the Country Music Hall of Fame® and Museum, is greatly enhanced by the building's design and materials. Throughout the 130,000-square-foot facility, symbolism expressed in the building's architectural and structural elements adds a subtle layer of storytelling to the visitor's experience.

For example, the building forms a massive bass clef when viewed from the air. Viewed from the front, the point on the building's sweeping arc suggests the tailfin of a 1959 Cadillac sedan, a favorite of many rockabilly and hard country singers. The building's front windows resemble piano keys. The tower on top of the Rotunda that extends down into the Hall of Fame is a replica of the distinctive diamond-shaped WSM radio tower, built in 1932 just south of Nashville and still in operation. In a broader sense, the building's tower symbolizes radio and television broadcasting. The tower also stretches skyward like a church steeple, recalling the role of religious culture in country music's history.

The Rotunda itself is replete with symbolic architectural elements. For example, the exterior of this cylindrical structure can be viewed variously as a drum kit, a rural water tower, or a grain silo. The four disc-shaped tiers of the Rotunda's roof evoke the evolution of recording media, from the 78-rpm record to the vinyl long-playing album, the 45-rpm single, and the compact disc. Stone bars on the Rotunda's outside wall symbolize the musical notes of the Carter Family's classic song "Will the Circle Be Unbroken," while the title of the song rings the interior of the structure. Hall of Fame member plaques are positioned within the Rotunda to resemble notes on a musical staff.

Solid, earthy materials native to the South—wood, concrete, steel, and stone—were used in the building's construction as reminders of the music's strong roots in the lives of working Americans. Southern yellow pine—like that used in the floors of southern warehouses and factories—adorns the floors of the majestic Conservatory and is also found in the Hall of Fame Rotunda and the Ford Theater. Crab Orchard stone from the East Tennessee mountains lends a homey, rustic touch to the Conservatory's "front porch" atmosphere and also lines the Rotunda's walls. The large steel beams supporting the Conservatory's glass ceiling and walls conjure images of railroads, a frequent subject of country songs. In another transportation metaphor, the cascading water along the Grand Staircase calls to mind the mighty rivers that have inspired so much of our nation's music and have physically connected musicians in various regions of the nation.

Musical symbolism continues within the museum galleries. Hardwood floors, show posters, curtain-like exhibit case fronts, and low-hanging lights suspended by cables create a backstage atmosphere on the third floor. Similarly, modular exhibit stations and vinyl floors evoke a recording studio environment on the second floor.

Exhibit Designer:
Ralph Appelbaum and Associates
Architect: Tuck-Hinton Architects, PLC

fun for *families*

Architecture

The building was designed to remind visitors about country music and its history. The shapes and building materials in the architecture bring to mind images of musical instruments and rural settings where country music began. Rural settings are places away from the city, out in the countryside.

How does the building make you feel? What building materials do you see in the floors, walls, and ceiling? What shapes or images do you see that remind you of musical instruments or of rural life in America? Some examples of things you might see are railroad tracks and bridges, piano keys, drums, or the frets of a guitar.

WHERE IS IT?

Kids' Activity
Areas
floor 3

Restrooms &
Changing Tables
floors 1 2 3

Water Fountains
floors 1 2 3

Restaurant
floor 1
*Kids menu and
coloring sheets
available*

Telephones
floor 1

FUN FOR FAMILIES

Look for " ⊕ " boxes throughout this book.

fun for
families

TIPS TO MAKE YOUR FAMILY VISIT A SUCCESS

1. Talk with your child about what to expect from a visit to a museum. Museums are great places for discovery.

2. There are many things to see in the museum, but don't overwhelm your child by trying to see everything. Keep in mind that if you look closely at everything, your visit could easily take three hours. Consider a two-day pass or a lunch break in the SoBro Grill downstairs.

3. Don't miss the Listening Stations and Touch-screen Interactive Computers scattered throughout the Museum. Hands-on children's activities and a kid's interactive computer program are located on the third floor. Hearing music and working with the computers bring the country music story to life for children—and adults too!

4. Bring a pencil and a sketchpad to record the fun and interesting things you see and hear.

5. Pick up a visitor guide brochure and a family brochure at the information desk upon your arrival. They include maps and activities for families.

Don't forget to go over the museum rules:

A. Walk, never run, through the museum.

B. Food, drink, and flash photography are not allowed in the galleries in order to protect the artifacts and exhibit materials.

C. If you have questions, please ask a Visitor Services Representative. They are stationed on each floor.

D. Families should always stay together when visiting the Museum. It is always helpful to have a meeting point in case you do get separated.

Questions to discuss with your child:

1. What is your favorite object, costume, or musical instrument in the exhibits?

2. What songs made you tap your feet?

3. What did you learn about country music that you didn't know before your visit?

SATURDAY WORKSHOPS AND FAMILY TOURS

Throughout the year, the Museum's Education Department offers workshops and tours for family visitors to explore ideas and themes related to country music. Programs are highly interactive and include learning experiences with artists, musicians, and music educators.

Saturday children's workshops—with hands-on instrument and costume activities—take place once a month. Call 615-416-2001 or check www.countrymusichalloffame.com for details.

ABOUT THE EDUCATION DEPARTMENT

The Country Music Hall of Fame® and Museum is a non-profit educational institution with a commitment to offering a variety of programs for students, educators, families, and the general public, focusing on history, music, visual art, architecture, and technology. Weekly instrument and songwriting demonstrations, monthly family workshops, and a variety of curriculum-based school programs, including the children's songwriting course *Words & Music*, highlight the Museum's offerings. Each year, more than seven thousand students and teachers participate in school programs, tours, and teacher workshops. In addition, more than two hundred community volunteers including more than sixty songwriters devote their time and talents to the Museum's educational programming and visitor services. These programs are designed to make curricular connections, inspire learning, and illustrate the story of country music.

For more information, contact the Education Department by phone, (615) 416-2001, or e-mail, education@countrymusichalloffame.com

HIGHLIGHTS
FROM THE
MUSEUM COLLECTION

Sing Me Back Home: A Journey Through Country Music is the title of the Country Music Hall of Fame® and Museum's permanent exhibit, an exciting, multi-layered journey through the life of country music. Through artifacts, photographs, original recordings, archival video, newly produced films, touchscreen interactive media, and beautifully rendered text panels, *Sing Me Back Home* immerses you in the history and sounds of country music, its meanings, and the lives and voices of many of its honored personalities.

TAKING THE JOURNEY

A SELF-GUIDED TOUR tour covering two floors of the Museum, *Sing Me Back Home* tells the story of country music from its pre-commercial roots in the nineteenth century through its vibrant life in the twenty-first century. **Organized chronologically**, the story moves through large subjects such as "Country During the War Years," while each glass artifact case has its own theme. You can read about the music and its makers if you like, or you can let the powerful photos, instruments, and beautiful costumes tell the story by themselves.

We encourage you to enjoy *Sing Me Back Home* at your own pace. As you take the journey, you will have many opportunities to step off the main path to explore the music in greater depth, or to hear some of those who have lived the story tell it in their own words. *Sing Me Back Home* is just what the title suggests: an exploration of the power of music to make history and to connect us to our deepest feelings.

"COUNTRY MUSIC IS THREE CHORDS AND THE TRUTH."
~ *Harlan Howard* ~

The Museum's story—and country's story—begins with the music's roots in the folk music of the British Isles, the folk music and blues of African-Americans, nineteenth-century gospel hymns, and the popular songs of the nineteenth and early twentieth century written by professional songwriters like Stephen Foster. In this opening of the Museum's main historical exhibit, evocative photographs, artifacts, and recordings convey the distinct strands of music and culture that intertwined to make up the fabric of country music.

Tip:

Artifacts and photos in the glass cases are accompanied by small, numbered buttons. Look for their corresponding numbers in the text panels.

1

Vaughan Quartets

Gospel hymns and harmony singing became fundamental building blocks of country music through publishers of Protestant hymnals, such as the James D. Vaughan Company in Tennessee and the Stamps-Baxter Company in Texas. These enterprising firms sent singing quartets across the South and Southwest to teach hymns—and to sell hymnals.

Handmade Banjo

Crude instruments like this late 1800s banjo—with its rough oak neck and drum of tanned ground-hog hide—suggest how important music was to America's rural communities in the years before commercially made instruments were easily available.

U.S. Soldiers from the Spanish-American War, ca. 1898

Guitars began to be mass-produced in America in the latter 1800s. Originally considered a parlor instrument for upper-class women, the guitar became a mainstay of country music. Key playing techniques, such as string bending and syncopated fingerpicking, came to country from African-American musicians.

Gospel Hymnal

This *Crowning Praises* gospel hymnal was published in 1911 by the James D. Vaughan Company of Lawrenceburg, Tennessee.

Nineteenth Century Sheet Music

The songs of professional songwriters of the 1800s greatly influenced the development of country. Stephen Foster, who wrote 189 published songs in his brief thirty-seven years of life, is the best known of these writers. Among his enduring songs that influenced country and folk music are "Jeanie with the Light Brown Hair," "Oh! Susanna," and "Camptown Races."

Country Music Milestones *like these appear on wall panels throughout the museum. The timeline shows landmark events in country music and places them in the context of American history.*

1877
Thomas Edison tests the first phonograph.

1900
The mandolin becomes the rage throughout urban America, with mandolin orchestras flourishing.

1904
The first double-sided records are issued.

1917
Cecil Sharp's book Folksongs from the Southern Appalachians *attempts to collect the musical notation and lyrics for southern traditional songs.*

1922
The country music recording industry begins, with recordings by Henry Gilliland and Eck Robertson in New York City.

BONNIE DODD
Resonator Guitar

Bonnie Dodd is an example of the many professional musicians who have performed and written country music without achieving the fame of a Jimmie Rodgers in the past or a Faith Hill today. Active from the 1920s to the 1950s, Dodd played this National resonator guitar on tour with Tex Ritter and as a featured act at KTHS in Hot Springs, Arkansas.

DEFORD BAILEY
Harmonicas and Megaphone

For fifteen years (1926-1941), DeFord Bailey was one of the most popular stars of Nashville's Grand Ole Opry, playing harmonica in a rhythmic, bluesy style all his own. He used the megaphone to control and amplify his sound. Sadly, country music's first black star didn't remain in the spotlight; he was fired from the Opry in 1941 under controversial circumstances that may have involved racism.

CORA CLINE
Dulcimer

Between 1928 and 1934, Cora Cline (the mother of nine children) regularly played her hammered dulcimer at the Grand Ole Opry, often joined by her husband, a fiddler. The handmade pine dulcimer was built circa 1900 by Irishman Lum Scott of New Roe, Kentucky.

fun for families

Instrument Search

How many different musical instruments can you find by looking at the exhibits and listening to the songs? How do the instruments change through time?

Instruments on display include: banjos, fiddles, mandolins, acoustic guitars, electric guitars, steel guitars, resonator guitars, drums, and at least one of the following— an autoharp, an electronic keyboard, a harmonica, a grand piano.

How many did you find of each instrument?

Early Record Sleeves

These 78-rpm record sleeves represent the wide range of record companies active in the 1920s and 1930s.

JIMMIE RODGERS
Guitar and Picture Disc

Jimmie Rodgers, known as "The Father of Country Music," was one of the music's first superstars, and he inspired hordes of talented musicians, including Gene Autry and Ernest Tubb. So popular was Rodgers that in 1928 the Weymann company of Philadelphia made this guitar expressly for Rodgers in exchange for his endorsement—one of the first artist endorsement deals in country music history. In another first, RCA Victor released this ten-inch, 78-rpm record—country's first picture disc—in June 1933, one month after Rodgers's death at age thirty-five.

CARTER FAMILY
Autoharp

Among the most legendary acts in the annals of country music, the Carter Family—Sara, A.P., and "Mother" Maybelle Carter—featured riveting Appalachian harmonies and Maybelle Carter's influential guitar work. The group first recorded in Bristol on the Tennessee-Virginia border in 1927, with Sara Carter playing this autoharp. Their career together continued until 1943, but their influence continues to this day.

DELMORE BROTHERS
Guitars

Alton and Rabon Delmore molded blues and country gospel into a lithe, driving harmony sound that influenced countless musicians who heard them on the Opry and other radio shows. Displayed are Rabon's 1942 018-T Martin four-string tenor guitar and Alton's 1940 000-18 Martin guitar, both of which went on public display for the first time in 2003.

1925
The term "hillbilly" is first used to describe commercial country music of the South, during an OKeh recording session in New York City.

1926
"Harmonica Wizard" DeFord Bailey becomes the Grand Ole Opry's most popular performer of the decade.

1927
Jimmie Rodgers and the Carter Family record tracks in a vacant hat warehouse for Ralph Peer in Bristol.

1933
Jimmie Rodgers dies.

CLAYTON McMICHEN
Trophy

Clayton McMichen's career is a good reminder of the considerable ambition, innovation, and talent of early country musicians. Raised in the Atlanta area, McMichen frequently participated in southern fiddling contests, winning more than a dozen times (the trophy was for first place in a 1929 competition). Though a key member of the Skillet Lickers stringband, he ultimately preferred jazz to country music, playing Dixieland in the forties and fifties.

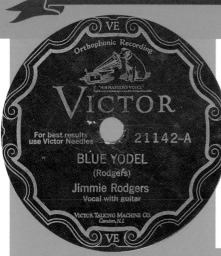

Listening Booths

Six "Sound in Your Mind" listening booths mark milestones in country music recording. Each booth allows you to hear in its entirety a landmark recording from the era explored in that section of the museum. Text panels inside explain the significance of each recording. By listening to all of the selected recordings, you can hear how the sound of country music has evolved over time.

BLUE YODEL
JIMMIE RODGERS

Recorded as an afterthought at his second recording session, "Blue Yodel" is the quintessential Jimmie Rodgers record and his first hit. A simple blues song, punctuated by Rodgers's loping, rhythmic guitar and exuberant yodeling, it sold more than half a million copies and influenced the style of innumerable artists, including Ernest Tubb, Jimmie Davis, Gene Autry, and Hank Snow. • • • • • • • • • • • • • • • • •

SLOWLY
WEBB PIERCE

Pedal steel guitars — steel guitars that used pedals to bend notes — were considered just a gimmick until Bud Isaacs played the newfangled instrument on this #1 country hit. Recorded on November 29, 1953, and topping the charts in early 1954, this leisurely love song established the pedal steel as a key ingredient in modern country music. ✳ ✳ ✳ ✳ ✳ ✳ ✳ ✳ ✳ ✳

GONE
FERLIN HUSKY

Ferlin Husky recorded "Gone" twice — once unsuccessfully as "Terry Preston" in 1952, and again in 1956 in this crossover hit version. The remake featured a rhythmic piano and an innovative vocal chorus that combined the Jordanaires quartet with soprano Millie Kirkham; this second version of "Gone" is often cited as the earliest instance of the Nashville Sound pop production style. • • • • • • • • • • • • • • • •

CRAZY ARMS
RAY PRICE

The Ray Price "shuffle" — a pulsing 4/4 rhythm driven by bass and fiddle — began with this huge 1956 hit. Propelled by a chugging bass line doubled by an acoustic stand-up bass and an electric bass guitar, "Crazy Arms" spent twenty weeks at #1 on the *Billboard* country charts, and it established a popular honky-tonk style that endures in country to this day. ✳ ✳ ✳ ✳ ✳ ✳ ✳ ✳ ✳ ✳ ✳ ✳ ✳ ✳ ✳ ✳

HE STOPPED LOVING HER TODAY
GEORGE JONES

George Jones's recording of this mournful ballad about a man who suffered from terminal heartache was the perfect marriage of singer, song, and producer. His aching vocal performance and Billy Sherrill's dramatic production squeezed every ounce of emotion out of the song. Its composers, Bobby Braddock and Curly Putman, captured the Country Music Association's Song of the Year award two years running, in 1980 and 1981.

HONKY TONK MAN
DWIGHT YOAKAM

Dwight Yoakam's first hit was a 1986 remake of a 1956 Johnny Horton hit, "Honky Tonk Man." In Yoakam's remake, Yoakam, guitarist/producer Pete Anderson, and the band duplicate yet subtly refashion the original vocals, beat, and lead-guitar part. In this way, Yoakam captures the raw urgency of the original record and translates it for a modern audience.

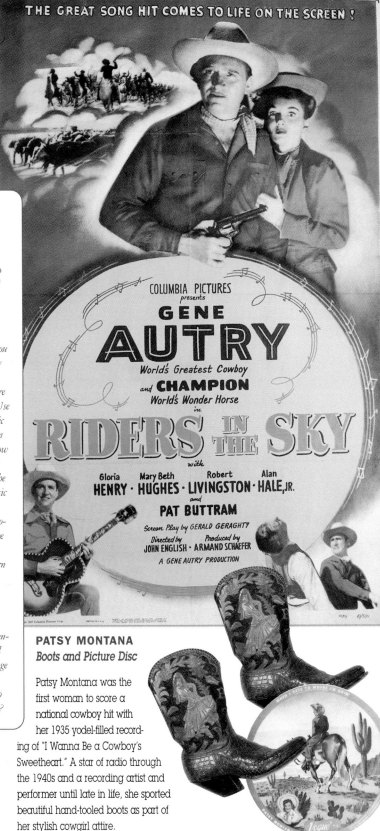

THE GREAT SONG HIT COMES TO LIFE ON THE SCREEN!

COLUMBIA PICTURES
presents

GENE AUTRY
World's Greatest Cowboy
and CHAMPION
World's Wonder Horse
in

RIDERS IN THE SKY

with

Gloria HENRY · Mary Beth HUGHES · Robert LIVINGSTON · Alan HALE, JR.
and
PAT BUTTRAM

Screen Play by GERALD GERAGHTY
Directed by JOHN ENGLISH · Produced by ARMAND SCHAEFER
A GENE AUTRY PRODUCTION

fun for families

Radio and Recordings

How and when do you listen to music? How do you think people listened to music before radios and stereos? Use the Touchscreen Music Station to listen to an early radio show. How does it sound to you?

Look at some of the records on which music was first recorded. Also, notice the phonograph that played the records. The sound came through the horn on the record player rather than through a speaker as it does today.

How did the invention of the radio and the phonograph change the music and the number of people who could hear the music?

PATSY MONTANA
Boots and Picture Disc

Patsy Montana was the first woman to score a national cowboy hit with her 1935 yodel-filled recording of "I Wanna Be a Cowboy's Sweetheart." A star of radio through the 1940s and a recording artist and performer until late in life, she sported beautiful hand-tooled boots as part of her stylish cowgirl attire.

BING CROSBY
78-rpm Records Album

Bing Crosby was one of country music's great popularizers. From the 1930s on, he recorded and enjoyed major pop hits covering such western fare as "Home on the Range," "The Last Round-Up," and "San Antonio Rose." This album of 78-rpm records was released in 1948.

GENE AUTRY
Guitar

Gene Autry was the first great singing cowboy star in western movies, ultimately making more than ninety pictures between 1934 and 1953. His career first gained momentum during his 1931–1934 stint at Chicago radio station WLS. While there, Chicago-based retailer Sears, Roebuck & Co. capitalized on Autry's already growing mass appeal as a cowboy singer by marketing this Gene Autry guitar for children.

1934
Gene Autry first appears in a movie, In Old Santa Fe.

1936
Ernest Tubb has his first recording session.

1937
Roy Rogers becomes Republic Studios' newest singing cowboy star.

1938
Roy Acuff, age thirty-four, joins the cast of the Grand Ole Opry.

PEE WEE KING
Accordion

Accordion player Pee Wee King and his Golden West Cowboys band joined the Grand Ole Opry in 1937, bringing visual flash and a smooth uptown sound to the down-home radio show before moving to Louisville radio and TV in the forties. In the fifties, he and sideman Redd Stewart scored major pop hits as cowriters of "The Tennessee Waltz," "You Belong to Me," and "Slow Poke."

"YOU ASK WHAT MAKES OUR KIND OF MUSIC SUCCESSFUL. I'LL TELL YOU. IT CAN BE EXPLAINED IN JUST ONE WORD: SINCERITY."
— *Hank Williams* —

HANK WILLIAMS
Nudie Suit and Boots

Undeniably the most significant figure in the history of country music, Hank Williams wrote and recorded such ageless songs as "Hey, Good Lookin'," "Your Cheatin' Heart," and "I'm So Lonesome I Could Cry." Often cutting a striking figure onstage, he had a distinctive wardrobe that included this famous suit made by Nudie the Rodeo Tailor. According to his friend Merle Kilgore, Williams had the suit with him when he died January 1, 1953, en route to a scheduled concert in Canton, Ohio.

TED DAFFAN
Turk Western Suit

When Ted Daffan was leading one of the West Coast's more popular country dance bands during World War II, he wore this sharp blue western outfit, designed by Nathan Turk. Since his heyday in the 1940s, Daffan is principally remembered as the author of such country standards as "Worried Mind," "I've Got Five Dollars and It's Saturday Night," and "Born to Lose."

ROSE MADDOX
Turk Dress

Rose Maddox and her brothers were known as "The Most Colorful Hillbilly Band in America" during the 1940s and 1950s thanks to dazzling costumes designed by Nathan Turk and their wild, freewheeling stage show that liberally mixed comedy and music. Rose Maddox's dress, made of gabardine and satin with embroidered roses, dates from the late 1940s.

1942
The Venice Pier opens, becoming the top western dance spot in Los Angeles.

1943
The Grand Ole Opry moves to the Ryman Auditorium.

1944
Eddy Arnold makes his first record.

22

BOB WILLS
Record Label and Fiddle

Born into a family of Texas fiddlers,
Bob Wills took country music in an exciting
new direction with his brand of western
swing, a danceable amalgam of country,
blues, pop, and jazz. After starring on Tulsa
radio for nearly a decade, he moved during
World War II to California, where he kept
dancehalls hopping and supplied radio
stations nationwide with pre-recorded shows
made for the Tiffany Transcription Company.

HANK THOMPSON
Fringed Jacket and Boots

A time-honored tradition among country stars has been to wear clothes designed around the theme of a popular song title. In 1948, singer Hank Thompson hit #2 on the charts with "Humpty Dumpty Heart," which inspired these boots designed by Nudie the Rodeo Tailor. The boots' embroidery was done by Viola Gae, a master embroiderer who did custom work for Nudie, Nathan Turk, and other costumers. The jacket is made of red and silver leather with rhinestone trim. The woman in this 1955 picture with Thompson is singer Wanda Jackson.

SPADE COOLEY
Fiddle

During the 1940s, Spade Cooley led a western swing band in Los Angeles that proved to be so competitive with Bob Wills that for a time Cooley (and not Wills) was known as "The King of Western Swing." Among Cooley's featured vocalists was future solo star Tex Williams. Cooley owned and played this fiddle with its distinctive headstock, decorated with the head of a Biblical apostle.

"COUNTRY MUSIC IS MUSIC WITH A LOT OF CLASS. IT'S JUST ORDINARY STORIES TOLD BY ORDINARY PEOPLE IN AN EXTRAORDINARY WAY."

∞ Dolly Parton ∞

MERLE TRAVIS
Guitar

A jack-of-all-trades, Merle Travis was an accomplished songwriter ("Sixteen Tons," "Smoke! Smoke! Smoke!"), influential fingerstyle guitar player, hit country singer, movie actor, and talented cartoonist. He designed one of the earliest solid-body electric guitars (pictured here), built by Paul Bigsby in 1947. It greatly influenced Leo Fender and other electric guitar makers.

01. 2-piece suit. Alligator theme embroidery. Rhinestoned shawl collar.

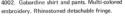

4002. Gabardine shirt and pants. Multi-colored embroidery. Rhinestoned detachable fringe.

4005. Western sport coat leather trim. Br buttons.

4003. White elastique suit. Gold metallic embroidery. Rhinestoned. Gold kid belt and buckle. White and gold boots, and customized hat.

4004. Suit with contrast piping and laced design. Custom boots to harmonize.

4007. White elastique suit. Embroidered ro and rhinestones. Custom tie.

NUDIE THE RODEO TAILOR

Shop Sign, Little Jimmy Dickens Jacket, Sewing Machine, and Catalog

Nudie the Rodeo Tailor was born Nutya Kotlyrenko in Kiev, in Russia, and immigrated to the United States at age eleven. After he opened his western wear shop in Hollywood in 1947, Nudie and his staff of talented designers (including son-in-law Manuel Cuevas) made costumes for stars ranging from Hank Williams to Elton John. (The sewing machine on display was used in the shop. A store catalog—not on exhibit—and eight catalog entries are shown here.) Along the way, Nudie introduced rhinestones to country music costumes. Though Nudie died in 1984, and the shop closed ten years later, the imprint of his visual flash endures.

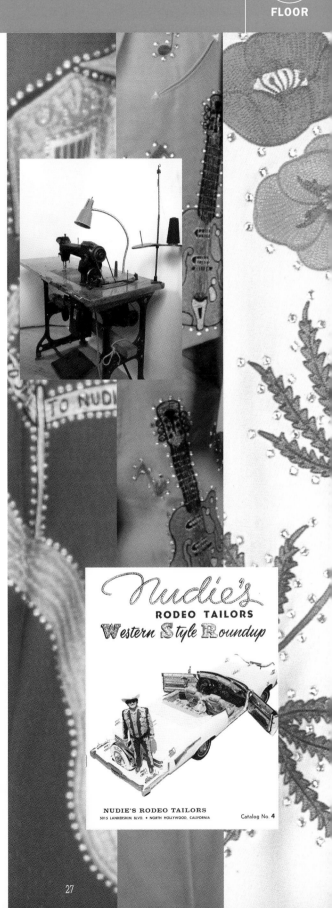

4006. Fleece jacket. Mouton collar and trim. Deerhorn buttons.

4008. Short jacket and pants/contrast color inlay and piping.

NUDIE'S RODEO TAILORS
5015 LANKERSHIM BLVD. • NORTH HOLLYWOOD, CALIFORNIA Catalog No. **4**

LEFTY FRIZZELL
Guitar

Lefty Frizzell, who enjoyed his first hits in 1950, influenced untold numbers of country singers with his drawling, note-bending vocal style. He also had a pronounced sense of visual style, playing this customized Gibson SJ-200 guitar.

1946
Hank Williams meets and begins working with Fred Rose.

1947
Ernest Tubb begins hosting a weekly live radio broadcast from the Ernest Tubb Record Shop in Nashville.

1949
Billboard *magazine retitles its "Hillbilly" music chart "Country and Western."*

1950
Lefty Frizzell is signed to Columbia Records.

1953
Hank Williams dies.

LEFTY FRIZZELL
Nudie Suit

Lefty Frizzell's sense of visual style extended to his stagewear. He was the first country singer to wear Nudie attire decorated with rhinestones, beginning in the early 1950s. (One of his Nudie suits from the mid-fifties is pictured.)

CARTER STANLEY
Guitar

RALPH STANLEY
Banjo

Though the Stanley Brothers began as Bill Monroe imitators in the late forties, they soon built their own distinctive version of bluegrass steeped in old-time stringband and gospel sounds. When Carter Stanley died in 1966, Ralph Stanley stepped out of his older brother's shadow and into the spotlight as a leading bluegrass singer, songwriter, and bandleader.

BILL MONROE
Mandolin

Bill Monroe turned the mandolin into a driving, rhythmic instrument, the perfect catalyst for his brand of high-powered acoustic music, which has come to be known as bluegrass—after Monroe's band, the Blue Grass Boys.

29

Jerry Lee Lewis was one of Sun Records' biggest rockabilly stars.

These rockabilly record jackets from the Hall of Fame archives suggest the jolt of youthful energy that rockabilly brought to music in the 1950s.

WANDA JACKSON
Fringed Dress

Wanda Jackson knew a thing or two about shaking the fringe. After briefly dating Elvis in 1955, she burst onto the rockabilly scene in the late fifties with torrid numbers like "Fujiyama Mama" and "Let's Have a Party." Though she later had bigger hits with straight-ahead country numbers like "Right or Wrong," her rockabilly records are still prized by collectors.

1954
George Jones, age twenty-two, makes his first records.

1955
Sam Phillips sells Elvis Presley's recording contract to RCA for $35,000.

1957
Buck Owens signs with Capitol Records in Los Angeles.

1958
The Country Music Association is chartered as a trade organization.

Waylon Jennings makes his first record.

Stereo LPs are introduced.

1961
Jimmie Rodgers, Fred Rose, and Hank Williams are the first to be elected to the Country Music Hall of Fame.

1962
Ray Charles records "I Can't Stop Loving You," selling 3 million records.

1963
Patsy Cline dies in a plane crash.

The Sunday **Star**
MAGAZINE OF THE WASHINGTON STAR · WASHINGTON, D. C. · MARCH 18, 1956

★ Meet the President's Docto

PATSY CLINE
Cowgirl Dress

Country music historians often cite Patsy Cline's classic recordings such as "Crazy" and "Sweet Dreams" as prime examples of the smooth, pop-oriented Nashville Sound. But Cline's own tastes tended toward more traditional country sounds and costumes, as evidenced by this cowgirl dress, which Cline's mother made for her. She died at age thirty in a 1963 plane crash west of Nashville.

JIM REEVES
Tuxedo Jacket

Jim Reeves epitomized the smooth Nashville Sound in the 1950s and 1960s with a warm baritone voice and hits that crossed over to the pop charts like "He'll Have to Go" and "Four Walls." Reeves's urbane sound was well-matched to this bright red tuxedo with black satin cuff, pocket, and lapel accents. He died at age forty in a 1964 Nashville plane crash.

MERLE HAGGARD
Nudie Suit

In a career marked by brilliant and sensitive songwriting and dozens of #1 records, Merle Haggard rarely wore dazzling rhinestone suits, preferring to let his music get the attention. Nevertheless, he ordered this one from Nudie the Rodeo Tailor in the late 1960s.

1963
The Country Music Association announces plans to build a Country Music Hall of Fame building.

1965
Charley Pride makes his first records.

1967
The Country Music Hall of Fame and Museum opens on Music Row.

1968
Conway Twitty records the first of his fifty #1 hits.

Country Music Foundation library opens at the Country Music Hall of Fame and Museum.

BUCK OWENS
Guitar

In 1966, through an agreement with Buck Owens, Sears, Roebuck & Co. began selling a line of "Buck Owens American" red, white, and blue guitars built by Gibson Guitar Corp. Roughly 30,000 of the Owens model guitars reportedly were sold, but the copy displayed in the Museum belonged to Owens himself (pictured left with the Buckaroos). He played a guitar like this one regularly on the long-running TV variety show *Hee Haw*.

RAY PRICE
Nudie Jacket

Hailing from Texas, Ray Price was known early in his career as the Cherokee Cowboy. In the late fifties and early sixties when so many country stars were flirting with pop crossover, Price focused on a danceable hard-country sound known as the shuffle, driven by twin fiddles and a propulsive walking bass.
Price scored thirty Top Ten country hits between 1952 and 1965. Afterwards, he proved he could cross over with the best of them with "For the Good Times."

CONNIE SMITH
Gown

Though small of stature, Grand Ole Opry star Connie Smith has consistently captivated audiences with her big alto voice and her emotional delivery of such hits as "Once a Day," "The Hurtin's All Over," and "Just One Time."

fun for families

Image

The image of a person is the way they appear to others. Many country singers (and performers in general) are concerned with the way that they look in the public eye. Examine Elvis Presley's "Solid Gold" Cadillac and Webb Pierce's Pontiac. What makes these cars different from most cars you see? What do these cars say about images of Elvis Presley and Webb Pierce? What kind of people do you think they were?

In the Archive Arcade, just ahead on this floor, find the Touchscreen Computer program for kids called Styles Onstage. Design a costume for a singer as you listen to one of their songs.

WEBB PIERCE'S CUSTOM PONTIAC BONNEVILLE

Webb Pierce could afford to show off. He had more #1 hits in the 1950s than any other country singer, thirteen in all. He paid Nudie the Rodeo Tailor $20,000 to customize his 1962 Pontiac Bonneville convertible. In addition to pistol door handles and steer horns on the front, more than one thousand silver dollars were used to ornament the car. The car was featured on the cover of Pierce's 1962 album *Cross Country*. Webb Pierce had a long friendship with Nudie, buying a new Nudie suit for every #1 hit he had. The suit on display commemorates "In the Jailhouse Now," #1 in 1955.

THE
ELVIS PRESLEY
ALBUM OF JUKE BOX FAVORITES
No. 1

ELVIS PRESLEY'S "SOLID GOLD" CADILLAC

Nicknamed the "Solid Gold" Cadillac and customized by George Barris, who also designed TV's Batmobile, Elvis's 1960 Cadillac Fleetwood 75 limousine includes gold-colored interior and gold records mounted on the roof interior. When Elvis ceased touring for several years in the 1960s, the Cadillac was sent out on tour in his place—and drew large crowds. The pictured souvenir book was sold during the tour.

ELVIS PRESLEY'S GOLD PIANO

This gilt grand piano, a gift to Elvis from his wife Priscilla, was a longtime fixture in his music room at Graceland.

CHET ATKINS
Guitar

"To me, getting a D'Angelico guitar was the equivalent of getting a Rolls Royce," Chet Atkins once wrote. "Mr. Guitar" played this 1950 D'Angelico on numerous recording sessions and in performance with the Carter Sisters. It is one of six Atkins axes in a special Museum display.

JOE MAPHIS
Guitar

Though a successful recording artist in his own right, Joe Maphis earned the admiration of numerous fellow musicians as a recording session guitarist. Whether onstage or in the studio, he turned heads with his lightning-speed picking on this double-necked guitar. Built for Maphis in 1954 by Semie Mosley, this was the first Mosrite guitar. In the 1960s, Mosrites became the signature guitar of the Ventures rock & roll instrumental band.

ROY ROGERS AND DALE EVANS
Lunchbox

As this 1950s lunchbox suggests, Roy and Dale were national stars. From the 1940s into the 1960s, Roy Rogers was America's most popular singing cowboy. Wife Dale Evans costarred with him in more than twenty movie westerns and on their long-running 1950s NBC-TV show.

fun for families

Collecting

The Museum collects important objects related to country music. The artifacts not on display are stored in movable storage units behind the glass wall within the exhibit. Museum curators ensure the safe storage and care of the artifacts so that they may be preserved for many years.

Why do you think the Museum collects and protects these artifacts? What objects do you collect? Why do you collect them?

Toy Pistol and Holster
Children's Book

Rogers shrewdly gained merchandising rights to his name in a movie contract negotiation and parlayed it into a wide array of merchandise, including lunchboxes, toy six-shooters, and storybooks.

The Precious Jewel

A select few musical instruments have become country music icons. Each reflects the unique spirit and personality of the artist who used it. Each seems to vibrate still with the strains of music embedded in the American soul.

These finely crafted creations of wood and metal were tools of the trade to the men and women who used them to make music. Today they are regarded as treasures. Some have been refinished, restored, or rebuilt. All made country music history and became powerful symbols in their own right.

Bill Monroe Mandolin

The most famous mandolin in American music history, Bill Monroe's Gibson F-5 Master Model is one of the finest stringed instruments ever made. Monroe bought the instrument in the early 1940s. In 1986, an intruder broke into Monroe's home and smashed the treasured mandolin with a fire-place poker. The instrument was painstakingly reconstructed from about 150 slivers of broken wood, and it remained Monroe's constant companion, onstage and in the recording studio, until his death in 1996.

Carter Family Guitar

In 1928, with money from the Carter Family's successful first recordings, Maybelle Carter paid $275 for the finest guitar she could find, this 1928 Gibson L-5. Until her death in 1978, she used it on hundreds of recordings, radio and television programs, and live appearances.

STOP LOOK and LISTEN

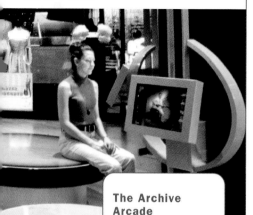

The Archive Arcade

The Archive Arcade consists of ten touchscreen computer monitors that allow visitors to sit, rest, and browse a menu of engaging interactive programs highlighting the holdings of the Museum's collections. Interactive programs focus on historic photos, rare records, and videos of classic comedy routines. A look at country costuming is designed especially for children (below).

3 FLOOR

fun for *families*

Welcome to the Country Music Hall of Fame's

Styles onstage for kids

Country costume styles often reflect the personalities, or the music, of the people wearing them. In this program you can design costumes based on the words in songs, the way some singers have done in the past.

"LONG TALL TEXAN"
LYLE LOVETT, 1996

Touch SONG LIST to design a costume using a different song.

Theaters

Included in the Museum tour are three movie theaters:

• The largest of the Museum's three theaters is the 213-seat **Ford Theater**, located on the lower level of the Rotunda. It is named for the Ford Motor Company.

1 FLOOR The Ford Theater offers special presentation films as well as an intimate venue for live performances, television and radio broadcasts, question-and-answer sessions with the stars, and educational demonstrations.

The Ford Division of the Ford Motor Co. is a Founding Partner of the new Country Music Hall of Fame® and Museum.

• **The Country Television Theater** provides an entertaining, informal history of country music on television, ranging from 1950s appearances by Hank Williams and Tennessee Ernie Ford, **3** FLOOR through 1960s favorites like The Porter Wagoner Show, to the impact of TNN, CMT, and awards shows featuring the likes of the Dixie Chicks and Faith Hill. The theater is located just past the Elvis Presley and Webb Pierce cars on the third floor.

• **The Star Experience Theater** explores singer Tim McGraw's life on the road, as captured during his 2000 "Soul2Soul" tour **2** FLOOR with wife Faith Hill. This theater, seating fifty-four people, is located in the middle of the second floor.

• **The Acuff-Rose Songwriter's Theater** takes its name from **2** FLOOR Nashville's first country music publishing company.

Established in 1942, Acuff-Rose Publications played a key role in the city's emergence as a music center. Hundreds of other publishers followed, and Nashville became known as the songwriting capital of the world.

Tip: Films run on a continual loop throughout the day. Check the countdown clock outside each theater for the beginning of the next show. Schedules of upcoming songwriters and musicians performing in the Museum, are posted throughout the Museum and at www.countrymusichalloffame.com

HEE HAW

Hosted by Buck Owens and Roy Clark, *Hee Haw* ran from 1969 to 1992, first on CBS-TV and then in national syndication. Its famous "Kornfield" set—out of which performers would pop up to tell the corniest of jokes—is now on display in the Museum along with costumes of *Hee Haw* favorites Archie Campbell, Grandpa Jones, Lulu Roman, Junior Samples, and Dave "Stringbean" Akeman.

1968
The first televised CMA Awards Show airs on NBC-TV.

1969
Hee Haw *and* The Johnny Cash Show *are launched on network television.*

1970
Merle Haggard dominates the CMA Awards, winning for single, album, male vocalist, and entertainer of the year.

fun for
families

Tip: A map listing the name and year
of every album on the wall is located
beside the wall on each Museum floor.

SHANIA TWAIN
THE WOMAN IN ME
MERCURY, 1995

Shania Twain burst to the forefront of the country music scene in 1995 with her second album, *The Woman in Me.* In 1996, it became the best-selling album ever by a female country artist, with more than 8 million copies sold. By mid-1999, this record-breaking figure had risen to 11 million.

JOHNNY CASH
JOHNNY CASH AT FOLSOM PRISON
COLUMBIA, 1968

Johnny Cash first immortalized California's Folsom Prison in 1956, with his Sun Records hit "Folsom Prison Blues." After he recorded his concert at Folsom on January 13, 1968, the song became a monster hit a second time, and country music gained one of its greatest live albums.

Wall of Gold Records

Three walls of the Museum contain every country-related album ever certified gold or platinum during the twentieth century: 854 records in all. The Recording Industry Association of America (RIAA) has been certifying these sales figures for recordings since 1958. Since 1976, albums selling more than 500,000 units have been certified gold; those selling more than one million are certified platinum.

Built into the walls on the third and second floors are twelve specially designed record frames that open to reveal additional information and to play a hit song from the album. Shown here are two of those interactive albums.

Changing Exhibits

As an active exhibition and research center, the Country Music Hall of Fame® and Museum is constantly staging new museum displays to highlight the diverse and continually evolving history of country music. Large changing exhibits, which are on display for various durations, are generally located at the beginning of the second floor, immediately after visitors leave the spiral staircase from the third floor.

Changing exhibits have included:

- Nashville Salutes Texas!: Country from the Lone Star State
  (May 2001-April 2002)
- Treasures Untold: Unique Collections from Devoted Fans (October 2002-April 2003)
- I'll Hold You in My Heart: The Eddy Arnold Collection (June 2003-December 2003)
- Night Train to Nashville: Music City Rhythm & Blues, 1945-1970
  (March 2004-December 2005)

DR. GEORGE W. BARKER
Harp-guitar

This Gibson harp-guitar from the 1920s, now part of the permanent collection of the Museum, was once owned by Dr. George W. Barker, a collector of odd and uncommon stringed instruments, most of them manufactured before World War II. A smalltown Georgia physician, he sometimes exchanged his medical services for relics similar to these. Barker's harp-guitar was displayed during *Treasures Untold*, an exhibit focusing on rare and unique items collected by music fans.

Owen Bradley's Office

"Crazy." "Coal Miner's Daughter." "Hello Darlin'." "I'm Sorry." All of these hits and more were produced by Owen Bradley, who set the highest standards for Nashville recordings during a lifetime of arranging and record producing. His office from the recording studio at Bradley's Barn in Mt. Juliet, Tennessee, is re-assembled in the Museum, just as he left it at his death in January 1998. Among the personal effects on view are musical arrangements, his electronic keyboard, gold record awards, and snapshots of artists he supervised, including Loretta Lynn, Brenda Lee, and Conway Twitty.

CINDY WALKER
Typewriter

Texas native Cindy Walker, a member of the Country Music Hall of Fame®, wrote timeless country hits such as "You Don't Know Me" on this lovingly decorated Royal typewriter, which was part of the *Nashville Salutes Texas!* Exhibition.

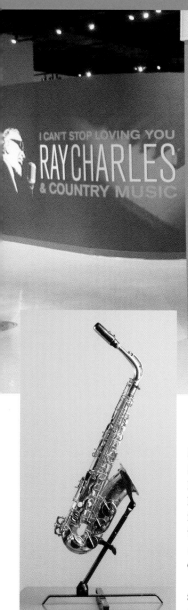

I Can't Stop Loving You: Ray Charles and Country Music, Sponsored by SunTrust offers an overview of Charles's legendary career, with special emphasis on his many contributions and connections to country music. He collaborated frequently with country stars, on national television and in the recording studio. His 1962 album *Modern Sounds in Country and Western Music* had a major impact on expanding country's urban audience.

Besides being a superb pianist, Charles was quite proficient on saxophone. He played this Selmer Super Action Alto Saxophone at nearly every live performance from the mid-1950s on.

Charles always appeared onstage in immaculately tailored clothes. His blindness required that he remain seated at the piano. To compensate for this lack of mobility, Charles wore flashy outfits that made him the undisputed focal point of his shows. He used garment bags like this one to transport stage outfits while on the road.

ROGER MILLER
Grammys

A songwriter and performer of rare and spontaneous wit, Roger Miller got his due in the mid-sixties, when he won an unprecedented eleven Grammy Awards for such across-the-board hits as "Dang Me," "Chug-a-Lug," and "King of the Road." His Grammys signaled that country had indeed hit the mainstream.

YOU'RE LOOKING at Country ~∞~ **THE OLD WAYS PREVAIL** ~∞~

LORETTA LYNN
Gown

Loretta Lynn told it like it was in the sixties and seventies in song after song from the woman's point of view. The coal miner's daughter had become country royalty by the time she wore this formal gown to a Washington, D.C., celebration for Roy Acuff years later.

1972
Emmylou Harris begins working with Gram Parsons, taking hard country to a new audience.

1974
President Richard Nixon joins the cast onstage to open the new Grand Ole Opry House.

1975
Thomas Hart Benton's painting The Sources of Country Music *is unveiled at the Country Music Hall of Fame.*

1976
Wanted! The Outlaws, *with Waylon Jennings, Willie Nelson, Jessi Colter, and Tompall Glaser, becomes country's first platinum album.*

1980
Alabama scores their first #1 single, "Tennessee River."

The movie Urban Cowboy *is released.*

1982
George Strait scores his first #1, "Fool Hearted Memory."

EMMYLOU HARRIS
Guitar

Plucked from obscurity by Gram Parsons in 1972, Emmylou Harris brought hard-country music to a wider audience while judiciously adapting rock elements into the mix. Harris's 1955 Gibson J-200 guitar was a trademark of hers for years, and it appeared on her 1979 LP *Blue Kentucky Girl.*

RAY CHARLES
Silk Jacket

A country fan since he listened to the Grand Ole Opry on radio as a boy, Ray Charles has recorded country songs in his own distinctive, r&b style throughout his career. "I felt it was the closest music, really, to the blues—they'd make them steel guitars cry and whine, and it really attracted me," he once said.

The Songwriter's Craft

Have you ever wanted to know how great songs get written? Where songwriters get their ideas? Visit any of the three touchscreen computer monitors beyond the Star Experience Theater to find out the answers to these questions and more. Through specially commissioned video interviews, Dolly Parton, Tom T. Hall, Mel Tillis, Harlan Howard, Matraca Berg, and Gary Burr answer selected questions and discuss the tricks of the songwriting trade and their most famous songs. Also displayed here are handwritten song lyrics of some of country's greatest hits.

POCKETFUL of Gold

⤳ **COUNTRY IN THE AGE OF PLENTY** ⤳

TRISHA YEARWOOD
Boots and Employment Application

Trisha Yearwood was a part-time college student and song demonstration, or "demo," singer when she filled out her 1986 application for work at the Museum. Five years later, she hit #1 with her first single, "She's in Love with the Boy." The boots bearing her initials were modeled after a pair of Hank Williams boots.

9/19/61

APPLICATION FOR
EMPLOYME

STEVE EARLE
Poster

Singer-songwriter Steve Earle bumped around Nashville for several years before making a name for himself with his stellar 1986 album *Guitar Town*. Though he struggled through drug addiction and a jail term in the early nineties, he emerged more musically prolific and respected than ever.

DWIGHT YOAKAM
Bolero Jacket and Jeans

In the mid-eighties, Dwight Yoakam helped lead the New Traditionalist pack back to a hard-country sound with a string of platinum albums and hit singles. Like his rough-edged music, his stagewear is a mix of country tradition and rock-star attitude.

JASON & THE SCORCHERS
Shirt and Hat

Jason & the Scorchers were the most successful of the "cowpunk" bands of the eighties, who blended the aggression of punk rock with the heart of hard-country. Lead singer Jason Ringenberg wore this fringed shirt on the cover of the group's groundbreaking *Fervor* EP in 1983.

1995
*Shania Twain
releases* The
Woman in Me, *
selling more albums
than any female
artist in country
music history.*

1997
*Garth Brooks hosts
more than 250,000
fans at his famed
Central Park
concert.*

1999
The Dixie Chicks'
Fly *debuts atop
country and pop
album charts.*

2000
*George Jones sur-
vives a near-fatal
car crash.*

*O Brother, Where
Art Thou? premieres
in movie theaters at
year's end.*

2001
*The Country Music
Hall of Fame and
Museum opens in
its new downtown
location.*

2002
*Six country music
albums top the
Billboard pop
chart. The artists:
Alan Jackson,
Kenny Chesney,
Toby Keith, the
Dixie Chicks,
Faith Hill, and
Shania Twain.*

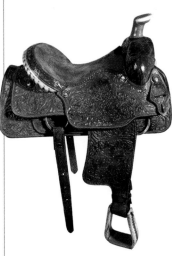

GEORGE STRAIT
Saddle

Balancing a love of traditional honky-tonk and western swing with a flair for romantic ballads, George Strait has been a leading artist since his 1981 major-label debut. A genuine cattle rancher and horseman, Strait received this hand-tooled leather saddle from his fan club in honor of his Entertainer of the Year awards in 1989 and 1990.

FAITH HILL
Dress

Since bursting onto the scene in 1993 with the #1 hit "Wild One," Faith Hill has become one of country music's best-known and most glamorous stars, with crossover hits like "Breathe" and "This Kiss" making her well known to pop music fans. Hill wore this champagne pink Gianni Versace dress on the "VH1 2000 Divas Live" cable television special.

2003
Johnny Cash died four months after the passing of his wife, June Carter Cash

2004
Gretchen Wilson's debut album, Here for the Party, *featuring "Redneck Woman," certified multi-platinum*

2005
Garth Brooks and Trisha Yearwood wed

EDDY ARNOLD: A LASTING LEGACY

As much as any artist, Eddy Arnold personifies country music's adaptation to the modern, urban world, and its transition from folk-based sounds, styles, and images to pop-influenced ones. Born into near-poverty on a west Tennessee farm in 1918, Arnold rose to fame on the strength of his talents as a singer, recording artist, and showman. Since 1945 he has sold some 85 million records, making classics of songs including "Bouquet of Roses," "The Cattle Call," and "Make the World Go Away." As a pioneering television performer and a leader in shaping the Nashville Sound, he helped win millions of new listeners for country music.

Arnold also played a vital role in preserving the history he helped create. In 2003, Arnold and his wife, Sally, gave their massive collection of career-related memorabilia to the Country Music Hall of Fame and Museum. The items displayed suggest the richness of that historic donation.

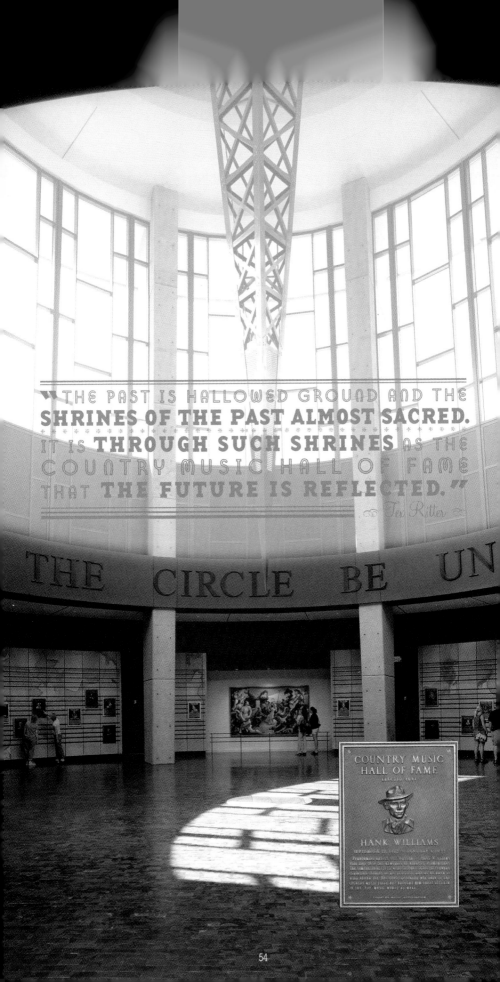

"THE PAST IS HALLOWED GROUND AND THE
SHRINES OF THE PAST ALMOST SACRED.
IT IS **THROUGH SUCH SHRINES** AS THE
COUNTRY MUSIC HALL OF FAME
THAT **THE FUTURE IS REFLECTED.**"

— *Tex Ritter*

THE CIRCLE BE UN

COUNTRY MUSIC
HALL OF FAME

HANK WILLIAMS

THE PINNACLE — THE COUNTRY MUSIC HALL OF FAME®

Election to the Country Music Hall of Fame® is the highest honor in country music. The Hall of Fame award was created in 1961 by the Country Music Association (CMA), the country music industry's leading trade organization. The award recognizes persons who have made outstanding contributions to country music over the length of their careers.

The Hall of Fame honors performers, songwriters, promoters, music publishing and recording leaders, broadcasters, and others in the music industry, reflecting country music's stature as both art and enterprise. New Hall of Fame members are selected annually by an anonymous panel of approximately three hundred electors, each of whom has been an active participant in the country music business for at least ten years and has made a major contribution to the industry. The CMA conducts the election, with winners honored during the televised CMA Awards Show each fall.

The first Hall of Fame members—Jimmie Rodgers, Fred Rose, and Hank Williams— were elected in 1961. Plaques representing each member were displayed at the Tennessee State Museum in Nashville until 1967, when the first Country Music Hall of Fame® and Museum building was opened on Music Row in Nashville. The plaques are now housed in the Hall of Fame Rotunda. Through a licensing agreement with the CMA, the Museum displays the plaques commemorating membership. The Country Music Hall of Fame® and Museum, as an institution, does not participate in the election process in any formal way.

his/her contribution to the advancement of country music and . . . the indelibility of his/her impact," a big part of which is considered to be "influence on others." Performers, songwriters, broadcasters, producers, and executives have all been honored, and though the listed criteria state that "it is not mandatory to honor the leaders in every activity related to country music," the CMA did stipulate that in 1989 and every third year thereafter "a non-performer will be inducted." Similarly, the CMA decided to induct a "Recording and / or Touring Musician" in 2003 and every third year thereafter.

Generally, one to four new members are inducted each year. From time to time since 1996, the CMA has created election categories specifically designed to admit deserving pioneers who have been overlooked in previous elections.

Through such a temporary modification in its election rules, the CMA was able to induct its largest group of members ever— twelve—in 2001. The special induction celebrated the opening of the new Country Music Hall of Fame® and Museum building.

fun for
families

Hall of Fame

The Country Music Hall of Fame honors many people who have helped in the success of country music. Singers, songwriters, comedians, and others are shown on the plaques. Find a plaque of a person also shown in another place in the Museum. Why is that person in the Hall of Fame? Why do you think we have a Country Music Hall of Fame? If you were going to be in a hall of fame for something, what would it be?

CRITERIA FOR ELECTION

Throughout the Hall of Fame's history, criteria for election have changed little. Only persons are eligible (individuals or groups, not companies, publications, broadcast stations, or other such entities), and the main qualities or achievements honored are defined in the election rules as "the degree of

NOMINATING AND VOTING FOR THE HALL OF FAME

Only a small portion of the CMA's approximately 6,100 members vote in the Hall of Fame process. The Hall of Fame Nominating Committee consists of twelve CMA members, each serving three-year terms. By secret ballot the Nominating

Committee chooses "no less than ten nor more than twenty" Hall of Fame candidates for each category that year, and these are submitted to the larger Panel of Electors. The Panel makes its selections in a two-stage process, first limiting each category to five final nominees. Winners since 1993 have been announced in the summer, well before the fall telecast, to help ensure that the honorees will be on hand.

's Spec Biggest to Date; Inaugurates "Hall of Fam

Hall of Fame a Reality with Groundbreaking

MAY 196

1966 MARCH

FIRST HALL OF FAME PLAQUES

The CMA Country Music Hall of Fame . . . A New Landmark of Distinction

NOVEMBER 196

The Road to the Hall of Fame

The Road to the Hall of Fame *outside the Hall of Fame Rotunda, provides a fitting prologue for visiting the Hall of Fame proper. Here two video monitors recap some of the special moments when country's finest were inducted into membership in the Hall of Fame. Selected clips include excerpts of acceptance speeches from Little Jimmy Dickens, Merle Haggard, Harlan Howard, George Jones, Grandpa Jones, Loretta Lynn, Willie Nelson, Minnie Pearl, Marty Robbins, Hank Snow, Floyd Tillman, Bob Wills, and Cindy Walker. In this area of the Museum, visitors can also trace major milestones in the history of the Country Music Hall of Fame® and Museum, from the election of its first members in 1961 to the original Museum's 1967 opening to the 2001 opening of the new Hall of Fame.*

COUNTRY MUSIC HALL OF FAME
ELECTED 1988

ROY ROGERS

THE HALL OF FAME ROTUNDA

The members of the Country Music Hall of Fame are country music's elite, and they are appropriately honored in a very special place in the Museum. The Rotunda is the Museum's most hallowed space and the final stop on the visitor's tour, the culmination of the Museum experience and of these great careers.

A soaring, majestic space commanding respect and reverence, the Rotunda is large, open, and skylit. The 5,300-square-foot hall stands seventy feet tall from its floor of southern yellow pine to its circle of clerestory windows admitting natural light. The likenesses of all the Hall of Fame members ring the walls of the Rotunda on bronze plaques, suspended on a metal framework like so many notes on a musical staff. The space is round to ensure that every Hall of Fame member is positioned in a place of equal importance. The title of the famous Carter Family song, "Will the Circle Be Unbroken," also rings the room, emphasizing the ongoing connectedness of country music's pioneers to its present.

Fittingly, American painter Thomas Hart Benton's priceless last painting, *The Sources of Country Music*, is permanently exhibited within the Hall of Fame Rotunda. Depicting the musical and cultural traditions that shaped country music and America, it is displayed alongside the images of the men and women who took those sources and created an original art form.

MEMBERS OF THE COUNTRY MUSIC HALL OF FAME®

(with years of induction)

1961 *Jimmie Rodgers*	1977 *Merle Travis*	1990 *Tennessee Ernie Ford*	2001 *Don Gibson*
1961 *Fred Rose*	1978 *Grandpa Jones*	1991 *Boudleaux and*	2001 *Homer & Jethro*
1961 *Hank Williams*	1979 *Hubert Long*	*Felice Bryant*	2001 *Waylon Jennings*
1962 *Roy Acuff*	1979 *Hank Snow*	1992 *George Jones*	2001 *The Jordanaires*
1964 *Tex Ritter*	1980 *Johnny Cash*	1992 *Frances Williams Preston*	2001 *Don Law*
1965 *Ernest Tubb*	1980 *Connie B. Gay*	1993 *Willie Nelson*	2001 *The Louvin Brothers*
1966 *Eddy Arnold*	1980 *Original Sons*	1994 *Merle Haggard*	2001 *Ken Nelson*
1966 *James R. Denny*	*of the Pioneers*	1995 *Roger Miller*	2001 *Webb Pierce*
1966 *George D. Hay*	1981 *Vernon Dalhart*	1995 *Jo Walker-Meador*	2001 *Sam Phillips*
1966 *Uncle Dave Macon*	1981 *Grant Turner*	1996 *Patsy Montana*	2002 *Bill Carlisle*
1967 *Red Foley*	1982 *Lefty Frizzell*	1996 *Buck Owens*	2002 *Porter Wagoner*
1967 *J. L. Frank*	1982 *Roy Horton*	1996 *Ray Price*	2003 *Carl Smith*
1967 *Jim Reeves*	1982 *Marty Robbins*	1997 *Harlan Howard*	2003 *Floyd Cramer*
1967 *Stephen H. Sholes*	1983 *Little Jimmy Dickens*	1997 *Brenda Lee*	2004 *Jim Foglesong*
1968 *Bob Wills*	1984 *Ralph Sylvester Peer*	1997 *Cindy Walker*	2004 *Kris Kristofferson*
1969 *Gene Autry*	1984 *Floyd Tillman*	1998 *George Morgan*	2005 *Alabama*
1970 *Original Carter Family*	1985 *Lester Flatt &*	1998 *Elvis Presley*	2005 *DeFord Bailey*
1970 *Bill Monroe*	*Earl Scruggs*	1998 *E. W. "Bud" Wendell*	2005 *Glen Campbell*
1971 *Arthur Edward Satherley*	1986 *Benjamin F. "Whitey"*	1998 *Tammy Wynette*	
1972 *Jimmie H. Davis*	*Ford (The Duke of Paducah)*	1999 *Johnny Bond*	*Throughout the main Museum*
1973 *Chet Atkins*	1986 *Wesley H. Rose*	1999 *Dolly Parton*	*tour, the exhibit displays featur-*
1973 *Patsy Cline*	1987 *Rod Brasfield*	1999 *Conway Twitty*	*ing Country Music Hall of*
1974 *Owen Bradley*	1988 *Loretta Lynn*	2000 *Charley Pride*	*Fame® members have text panels*
1974 *Frank "Pee Wee" King*	1988 *Roy Rogers*	2000 *Faron Young*	*bearing bronze Hall of Fame*
1975 *Minnie Pearl*	1989 *Jack Stapp*	2001 *Bill Anderson*	*symbols.*
1976 *Paul Cohen*	1989 *Cliffie Stone*	2001 *The Delmore Brothers*	*For biographical information*
1976 *Kitty Wells*	1989 *Hank Thompson*	2001 *The Everly Brothers*	*on Hall of Fame members, visit the Hall of Fame's web site at www.countrymusichalloffame.com*

THE LAST PAINTING OF AN AMERICAN MASTER:
The Sources of Country Music by Thomas Hart Benton

Country music has always evoked a host of images—a train on the horizon, sounding its lonely whistle; a riverboat headed upstream toward new adventures; a cowboy on the range. These images—and many more from America's past—can be seen in Thomas Hart Benton's *Sources of Country Music*, a painting that celebrates the roots of country music and the pioneer history of America. The last great work of an American master, Benton's *Sources of Country Music* was commissioned in 1973 by the Country Music Hall of Fame® and Museum. Today the six-foot-by-ten-foot acrylic-on-canvas mural is accorded a place

of honor, hanging in the Hall of Fame Rotunda of the new Country Music Hall of Fame® and Museum, among the plaques recognizing country music's greats.

Benton was well chosen by the Hall of Fame to create a painting on country music's roots. He was himself a skilled harmonica player—in 1941 he had made six recordings for Decca Records issued as the 78-rpm album *Saturday Night at Tom Benton's.* Trained in Paris amidst the Cubists and the Impressionists and based for much of his life in New York City, Benton became known for his devotion to Americana and the simple, rural, small town life depicted in his art. *The*

Sources of Country Music touched on a number of Benton's own influences and interests: his musical upbringing, his earlier artistic themes and subjects, and his notions of democratic art and its accessibility to the common man (he wanted this to be "a work aimed at persons who do not ordinarily visit art museums").

Benton worked at the painting steadily from the fall of 1973 until his sudden death from a heart attack in January 1975. The Sources of Country Music proved to be Benton's final work, and it was virtually complete, save for a coat of varnish and his signature.

I believe I have wanted, **more than anything else,** to make pictures, the imagery of which would carry unmistakably **American meanings** for Americans and **for as many of them** as possible. 99 — *Thomas Hart Benton, 1951*

In March 1975, the Country Music Foundation® took delivery of the mural from Benton's estate, and that July the painting was formally unveiled at the Museum. Over the years, it has remained one of the Museum's more popular exhibits. The Sources of Country Music is indeed a fitting and worthy last painting by one of America's greatest artists.

Benton Studies

Because the Country Music Hall of Fame® and Museum commissioned the painting, and because it was Benton's last work, the Museum owns the most complete collection of preliminary materials related to any of Benton's works. In addition to his ongoing correspondence with Hall of Fame officials as the mural took shape, there are Benton's preliminary drawings in pen and ink (now also the property of the Hall of Fame), and the plasticene figurines he used as models, each representing one of the images he would commit to canvas. There was even a documentary film of the work in progress, with footage from a camera that was literally looking over Benton's shoulder as the canvas filled. Benton's own comments about the work were added to the soundtrack. Today, these preliminary sketches, models, and the documentary film are used in the Museum's educational programs.

FRIST LIBRARY AND ARCHIVE

The Country Music Hall of Fame® and Museum is one of the largest and most active popular music research centers in the world. To collect, preserve, and convey the history of country music, the Country Music Hall of Fame® and Museum has assembled what is generally considered to be the world's largest and finest collection of materials related to country music.

As visitors pass through the Museum, this collection is on view in the central, glass-enclosed core of the building. Here the Museum's vast holdings are housed, and archival and curatorial staff can be seen going about the daily process of preservation and study that is the essence of the Museum.

The architects and exhibit designers created the two-story glass vault to expose the archive and its research, an integral part of the museum experience. The vault also includes a visible state-of-the-art audio studio for re-mastering sound recordings and recording live concerts in the Museum's Ford Theater. The audio studio is internationally known for preserving historical recordings, and it plays a key role in the production of the Museum's many important country music reissues.

The heart of the Museum's collection is the massive record collection of 200,000 sound recordings, including cylinders, 45s, 78s, LPs, and CDs. These recordings virtually span the history of recorded sound and encompass rare recorded radio programs, demonstration recordings (demos), recordings of live radio broadcasts of the Grand Ole Opry, and numerous radio programs made for mass distribution. The collection of pre-World War II country recordings is as complete as any in the world. The entire record collection is constantly expanding to document the ongoing history of country music.

Other highlights of the Museum's holdings include:

- over 800 stage costumes
- over 600 musical instruments
- some 1,000 oral history interviews with performers on audiotape
- some 2,500 advertising posters
- nearly 5,000 motion pictures and videotapes
- some 6,000 pieces of published sheet music and 3,000 songbooks
- more than 60,000 photographs

The Library also houses an extensive book and periodical collection, encompassing more than 8,000 books and nearly 1,000 periodical titles. Thousands of organized newspaper clippings and microfilmed documents round out the collection.

Besides allowing the Museum staff to assemble accurate and interesting exhibits, these collections also inform and undergird the Hall of Fame's many books (CMF Press) and historic reissue recordings (CMF Records). Finally, many of these collections are available for study in the Hall of Fame's library reading room, which is open by appointment to journalists, teachers, students, performers, music business professionals, and any others interested in the study of country music. To make an appointment, call the reference librarian at 615-416-2001.

HOME OF THE HITS: HISTORIC RCA STUDIO B

There is probably no other studio in Nashville that can claim the number of hit records that have come from Studio B, operated by RCA Records from 1957 to 1977. Here is where some of country's most celebrated performers recorded, including Elvis Presley, Charley Pride, Chet Atkins, the Everly Brothers, Roy Orbison, Porter Wagoner, Waylon Jennings, Willie Nelson, Dolly Parton, and many more. Over 35,000 songs were brought to life at Studio B. Inside you can almost feel the walls come alive with the echoes of some of country's favorite melodies.

Built in 1957, Studio B is the oldest surviving recording studio in Nashville. In the 1960s, it became known as the cradle of the "Nashville Sound," a relaxed, yet polished pop-country style that helped to revive the popularity of country music

Eddy Arnold at RCA's Studio B.

while establishing Nashville as an international recording center. For many years, Hall of Famer Chet Atkins managed RCA's Nashville operation and produced hundreds of hits in Studio B.

The Country Music Hall of Fame® and Museum began operating Studio B as a historic site in 1977 and in 1996 restored the primary studio area to its vintage look. Facilitated by the philanthropy of the Mike Curb Family Foundation, Belmont University students use Studio B as a workshop for recording projects, a partnership that helps support the Museum's educational programs.

Studio B tours are offered daily and depart from the Country Music Hall of Fame® and Museum. Call 1-800-852-6437 for more information.

Connie Smith

HITS RECORDED AT RCA'S STUDIO B:

Eddy Arnold — "Tennessee Stud"	Dolly Parton — "Jolene"
Bobby Bare — "Detroit City"	Elvis Presley — "Are You Lonesome Tonight?"
Skeeter Davis — "The End of the World"	Jim Reeves — "He'll Have to Go"
Everly Brothers — "All I Have to Do Is Dream"	Connie Smith — "Once a Day"
Roy Orbison — "Only the Lonely"	Hank Snow — "I've Been Everywhere"

HATCH SHOW PRINT

Hatch Show Print, one of the oldest working letterpress poster print shops in America, is owned and operated by the Country Music Hall of Fame® and Museum. The firm was founded

by C. R. and H. H. Hatch in 1879 and blossomed in the 1920s under the steady hand of Will T. Hatch, who applied his own bold style in hand carving the wood blocks used in the letterpress process. For much of the twentieth century, the firm's vibrant, colorful posters served as a leading advertising medium for southern entertainment—from vaudeville and minstrel shows, to magicians and opera singers, to Negro League baseball games and B-movies. Many of Hatch's most loyal clients were Grand Ole Opry stars. To this day, Hatch posters for Bill Monroe, Roy Acuff, and others are cherished by country fans, designers, and art critics alike.

Each Hatch Show Print poster is a unique creation, individually handcrafted and inked onto paper in a painstaking process that dates back to the Gutenberg Bible in the fifteenth century. This process, known as letterpress, involves inking hand-carved wood blocks and metal photo plates and type, which are then pressed to paper to form an image. The shop that produces these colorful posters has long been a downtown Nashville landmark and the guardian of a very special piece of Americana. Owned by the Country Music Hall of Fame® and Museum since 1992, Hatch Show Print not only maintains the original hand-carved wood blocks and massive old letter presses for producing restrikes of classic designs, but also creates bold new posters for contemporary entertainers that continue the venerable firm's artistic traditions.

This Nashville institution is open to the public 9 a.m. to 5 p.m., Monday through Friday, and 10 a.m. to 5 p.m. Saturdays. It's located at 316 Broadway, two blocks north of the Museum. For those eager to know more, *Hatch Show Print: The History of a Great American Poster Shop*, a lavishly illustrated book chronicling the history of the poster shop, is available in the Museum Store and at good bookstores nationwide.

MUSEUM STORE

Where can you find one of the largest country music and book selections in the region? It's all at the Hall, of course! Located

up front, on the Fifth Avenue side of the Museum, the 6,500-square-foot store offers a wide variety of merchandise sure to please music lovers of all ages. Stop by the Museum Store to browse through our huge selection of compact discs, videos, and books.

And don't forget our full range of Country Music Hall of Fame® official logo apparel and souvenirs. No ticket needed to shop! Or visit the Hall's online store for convenient at-home shopping: www.countrymusichalloffame.com

And while you're browsing in the Museum Store, don't miss the live radio broadcasts from the **XM Satellite Radio** studio, featuring music and live interviews.

SOBRO GRILL

Named for the Museum's location SOuth of BROadway, SoBro Grill and SoBro2Go offer visitors a variety of mealtime options in the

casual, sunlit atmosphere of the Curb Conservatory. SoBro Grill serves up a contemporary spin on some of the greatest hits of southern cuisine. SoBro2Go offers snacks, sweets, and beverages seven days a week during museum operating hours. The SoBro Grill serves lunch 11 a.m. to 2:30 p.m. Monday to Saturday. SoBro2Go is open 9 a.m. to 5 p.m. daily for takeout.

PLANNING A SPECIAL EVENT

Looking for a new and unique place to stage your special event? Treat your guests to a wonderful evening of fun and discovery at the Country Music Hall of Fame® and Museum. From casual receptions to black tie galas, the Country Music Hall of Fame® and Museum is the perfect setting. We have entertained corporate and convention clients, university alumni, and Nashville superstars. We offer a full range

of event management services, including food and beverage service, live entertainment, keepsake gifts, invitations, and docent tour guides. Ask for the Event Sales and Marketing Manager at 615-416-2001 or visit www.country-musichalloffame.com for more information.

Kids menu and coloring sheets available

fun for families

CMF PRESS

The Country Music Hall of Fame® and Museum's publishing activity falls into three main areas. First, in cooperation with major trade publishing houses, the Museum produces a variety of commercial titles, such as the authoritative reference guide *The Encyclopedia of Country Music*, published by Oxford University Press. Second, in cooperation with Vanderbilt University Press, the Hall of Fame publishes in-depth historical and biographical studies, such as *Heartaches by the Number: Country Music's 500 Greatest Singles* and *Singing in the Saddle: The History of the Singing Cowboy*. Lastly, the Museum's own in-house magazine, the *Journal of Country Music*, has been the leading

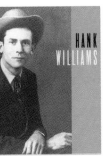

serious periodical covering country music since its inception in 1971. It is available at better bookstores nationwide and by subscription. You can subscribe or purchase back issues at www.countrymusichalloffame.com.

CMF RECORDS

The Country Music Hall of Fame® and Museum's record label has been involved since the late 1970s in the reissue of classic recordings. Functioning as a producer and packager, the Museum has compiled more than sixty-five historical sets for release on various major record labels, including such high-profile CD boxes as *The Patsy Cline Collection; The Complete Hank Williams;* and *From Where I Stand: The Black Experience in Country Music.* Since 1985, CMF Records has issued its own recordings as well, focusing on significant tracks that have been overlooked by commercial recording companies. These include classic performances by such legendary artists as Hank Williams, Webb Pierce, Jimmy Martin, and Johnny Paycheck. Hall of Fame-produced recordings have been nominated for numerous awards including seven Grammys. *The Complete Hank Williams* won two 1998 Grammys: Best Historical Album and Best Boxed Recording Package. *Night Train to Nashville: Music City Rhythm & Blues, 1945-1970* won the 2004 Grammy for Best Historical Album.

MUSEUM MEMBERSHIP AND GIVING OPPORTUNITIES

Become a member and help support the Museum and its programs.

Members of the Museum receive the following benefits:

- Collectible membership card
- Complimentary one-year general admission
- 15 percent discounts at the Museum Store, SoBro Grill, and Hatch Show Print
- Invitations and notices for special events

Help the Museum tell country music's

story by making a financial contribution.

Call 615-416-2001 or visit our web site at www.countrymusichalloffame.com to start your membership and to learn more about giving opportunities.

Accredited by the American Association of Museums, the Country Music Hall of Fame® and Museum is a Section 501(c)3 non-profit educational organization. All donations are tax-deductible to the full extent of the law. Consider including the Country Music Hall of Fame® and Museum in your estate planning.

E-NEWSLETTER

Be sure to sign up at www.countrymusichalloffame.com to receive our e-newsletter, a personal guide to events and programs at the Country Music Hall of Fame® and Museum. Highlights will include information on exhibit openings, concerts, monthly family programs, updates on weekly museum programming, membership information, and so much more!

"WE CAN'T **KNOW** WHERE WE'RE GOING UNTIL WE KNOW **WHERE WE'VE BEEN** .

AND THE **MUSIC OF THE PAST** IS NOT JUST TO STUDY AND PUT IN A MUSEUM.

THE WAY TO STUDY IT IS **TO PUT IT ON THE STEREO** AND TURN IT UP AS LOUD AS YOU CAN. "

Emmylou Harris